Directions

Cut out all the figures and

* Paste them following the composition of each artwork or

* Create your own collage!

Dare to add variations, change the order, the composition or add new elements such as pieces of newspaper, paint... This book is designed for you to lose the fear of your own creativity and discover yourself in the process.
Let yourself be surprised!

- You can paste your work on any surface: colored cardboard, wood, paper previously painted by you...
At the end of the book, some plain colored sheets are included.

- For a more impressive finish, instead of gluing the figures directly, add a small piece of cardboard, eva rubber or anything with a little thickness, so your work will be in 3 dimensions and it will be even more spectacular!

- When you have finished, you can frame it and enjoy your great work of art every day. Congrats!

El Katif
Ras
Medna
erayah
El Hassa
Yemama
Yembo
Sherm Rhab
B
I
Morr
Kolbe
Drida
Mekka
Houke
Leat
Koomfidah
Berber
Gurkab
Has
Dof
Medwah
Shendy
Dhalac
Gaitha
ghawa
Arkee
Suggen
tak
MEROE
Abou Khara
Loheia
Hodeida
Makallah
Mocha
Taka
GONDAR
Angot
Aden (B
GULF OF ADEN
Socotra
Tamar
Obeid
Perim
ABYSSINA
Bab el Mandeb
Der
AMHARA
Magdala
Zeyla
(B.)
C.Gu
Fades
Mekan
Hurrur
Somauli
Hafowa
Bertat
Dand
Ras Mabl
Port
Nile
Korchassi
Auxa
Ras al Khy
Adael
Kaffa
GALLAS
Gondokoro
Shiwelh
Ras Asso
Obbo
SOMAULI
Murchison
Shitu
Barbo
Magadoxo
Jillip
Torra
Brava
Jubo

El Katif
El Hassa
Yemama
Medina
Ras
Yembo
Sherm Rhab
Mekka
Dralal
Leat
Koomfidah
Morr
Kolbe
Kouke
Berber
Gurkab
Shendy
Arkeeko
Dhalac
Loheia
Hodeida
Makallah
MEROE
AbouKhara
Mocha
Aden
GULF OF ADEN
Socotra
ABYSSINI
AMHARA
Mugdala
Leyla
Barboni
SOMALI
Ras Mabb
Hurrur
Dand
Anva
Ras al Khy
Korchassi
Kaffa
Shiweh
Ras Asso
GALLA
Gondokoro
Obbo
Brava
Torra
Filip
MACADOXO
Magadoxo
Juba

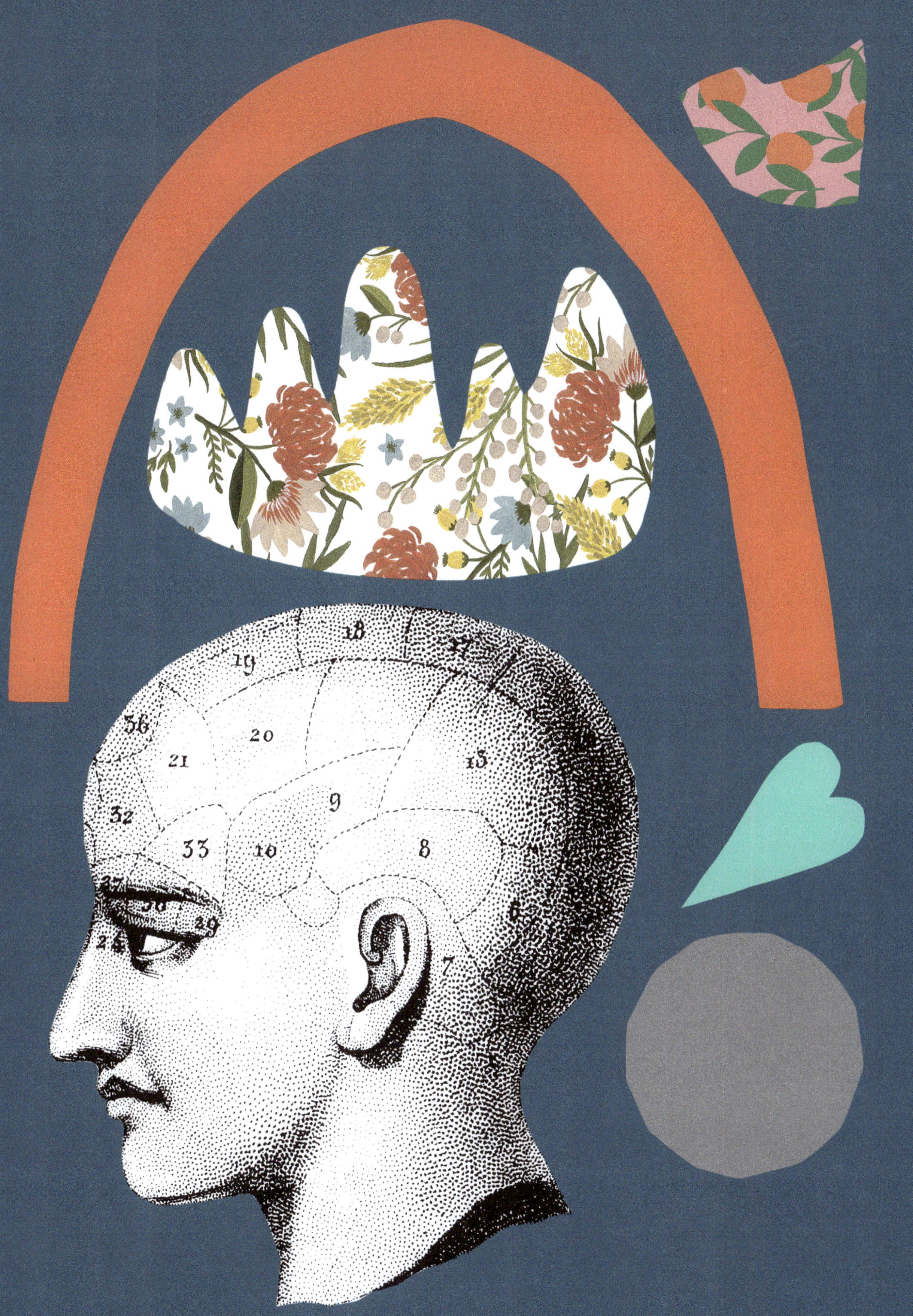